Student: ______________________

TPRI®

# Progress Monitoring for Emergent Readers™ (PMER)

## Student Record Sheet Kindergarten

I0737530

ISBN-13: 978-1-59857-133-2
ISBN-10: 1-59857-133-8
90000>
9 781598 571332



Paul H. Brookes Publishing Co., Inc. 1-800-638-3775 www.brookespublishing.com

**Student:** ______________________________

## Required

### Letter Name/Letter Sound

*Discontinue scoring when student misses 5 letter sounds in a row.*

| Item | Set 2 | | Set 4 | | Set 6 | | Set 8 | | Set 10 | | Set 12 | |
|---|---|---|---|---|---|---|---|---|---|---|---|---|
| | Name (0,1) | Sound (0,1) | Name (0,1) | Sound (0,1) | Name (0,1) | Sound (0,1) | Name (0,1) | Sound (0,1) | Name (0,1) | Sound (0,1) | Name (0,1) | Sound (0,1) |
| 1. S s | | | | | | | | | | | | |
| 2. T t | | | | | | | | | | | | |
| 3. B b | | | | | | | | | | | | |
| 4. K k | | | | | | | | | | | | |
| 5. A a | | | | | | | | | | | | |
| 6. P p | | | | | | | | | | | | |
| 7. C c | | | | | | | | | | | | |
| 8. J j | | | | | | | | | | | | |
| 9. O o | | | | | | | | | | | | |
| 10. Z z | | | | | | | | | | | | |
| 11. D d | | | | | | | | | | | | |
| 12. V v | | | | | | | | | | | | |
| 13. M m | | | | | | | | | | | | |
| 14. G g | | | | | | | | | | | | |
| 15. L l | | | | | | | | | | | | |
| 16. E e | | | | | | | | | | | | |
| 17. F f | | | | | | | | | | | | |
| 18. N n | | | | | | | | | | | | |
| 19. R r | | | | | | | | | | | | |
| 20. Q q | | | | | | | | | | | | |
| 21. H h | | | | | | | | | | | | |
| 22. U u | | | | | | | | | | | | |
| 23. W w | | | | | | | | | | | | |
| 24. I i | | | | | | | | | | | | |
| 25. X x | | | | | | | | | | | | |
| 26. Y y | | | | | | | | | | | | |
| TOTAL | | | | | | | | | | | | |

## Required

### Letter Name/Letter Sound

*Discontinue scoring when student misses 5 letter sounds in a row.*

| Item | Set 14 | | Set 16 | | Set 18 | | Set 20 | | Set 22 | | Set 24 | |
|---|---|---|---|---|---|---|---|---|---|---|---|---|
| | Name (0,1) | Sound (0,1) | Name (0,1) | Sound (0,1) | Name (0,1) | Sound (0,1) | Name (0,1) | Sound (0,1) | Name (0,1) | Sound (0,1) | Name (0,1) | Sound (0,1) |
| 1. S s | | | | | | | | | | | | |
| 2. T t | | | | | | | | | | | | |
| 3. B b | | | | | | | | | | | | |
| 4. K k | | | | | | | | | | | | |
| 5. A a | | | | | | | | | | | | |
| 6. P p | | | | | | | | | | | | |
| 7. C c | | | | | | | | | | | | |
| 8. J j | | | | | | | | | | | | |
| 9. O o | | | | | | | | | | | | |
| 10. Z z | | | | | | | | | | | | |
| 11. D d | | | | | | | | | | | | |
| 12. V v | | | | | | | | | | | | |
| 13. M m | | | | | | | | | | | | |
| 14. G g | | | | | | | | | | | | |
| 15. L l | | | | | | | | | | | | |
| 16. E e | | | | | | | | | | | | |
| 17. F f | | | | | | | | | | | | |
| 18. N n | | | | | | | | | | | | |
| 19. R r | | | | | | | | | | | | |
| 20. Q q | | | | | | | | | | | | |
| 21. H h | | | | | | | | | | | | |
| 22. U u | | | | | | | | | | | | |
| 23. W w | | | | | | | | | | | | |
| 24. I i | | | | | | | | | | | | |
| 25. X x | | | | | | | | | | | | |
| 26. Y y | | | | | | | | | | | | |
| TOTAL | | | | | | | | | | | | |


Paul H. Brookes Publishing Co., Inc. 1-800-638-3775 www.brookespublishing.com

## Set 4 — Required

| Listening Comprehension | Score (0,1) |
|---|---|
| **1. Why was Jessica's class stuck inside all day?**<br>Answer: It was raining. | |
| **2. What were Jessica's brother and cousins doing while she was lying on the couch?**<br>Answer: Playing video games. | |
| **3. What does the word *pouring* mean in the sentence, "It was *pouring* rain."  *pouring***<br>Answer: It was raining very hard. | |
| **TOTAL** *(3 possible)* | |

## Set 4 — Optional

| Rhyming | Score (0,1) |
|---|---|
| **1. mad, add** | |
| **2. scout, pout** | |
| **3. lock, rock** | |
| **4. blast, past** | |
| **5. tin, bin** | |
| **TOTAL** *(5 possible)* | |

## Set 6 — Required

| Listening Comprehension | Score (0,1) |
|---|---|
| **1. The next time they visit the zoo, what animal do you think Taylor and her grandparents will see first?**<br>Answer: An elephant. | |
| **2. What kind of chairs did Grandma, Grandpa and Taylor sit on when they ate lunch?**<br>Answer: Chairs shaped like animals. | |
| **3. What does *muggy* mean in the sentence, "It was hot and *muggy* inside the forest." *muggy***<br>Answer: Warm; humid. | |
| **TOTAL** *(3 possible)* | |

## Set 6 — Optional

| Rhyming | Score (0,1) |
|---|---|
| 1. wire, hire | |
| 2. ball, fall | |
| 3. Sam, ham | |
| 4. ten, den | |
| 5. red, bed | |
| **TOTAL** *(5 possible)* | |

**Blending**

| Item | Answer | Score (0,1) |
|---|---|---|
| 1. /sun/ /shine/ | sunshine | |
| 2. /black/ /board/ | blackboard | |
| 3. /snow/ /ball/ | snowball | |
| 4. /vis/ /it/ | visit | |
| 5. /clev/ /er/ | clever | |
| | **TOTAL** *(5 possible)* | |


Paul H. Brookes Publishing Co., Inc. 1-800-638-3775 www.brookespublishing.com

## Set 8 — Required

| Listening Comprehension | Score (0,1) |
|---|---|
| **1. Why did four of the fish die?**<br>Answer: They were fed too much food. | |
| **2. Why does the person telling the story want to learn more about fish and aquariums?**<br>Answer: To prove to mom he/she can take care of the fish so he/she can get more fish. | |
| **3. What does the word *responsibility* mean in the sentence, "I now know that having an aquarium is a big *responsibility*." *responsibility***<br>Answer: To be in charge of. | |
| **TOTAL** *(3 possible)* | |

## Set 8 — Optional

| Rhyming | Score (0,1) |
|---|---|
| **1. joy, boy** | |
| **2. dug, rug** | |
| **3. van, man** | |
| **4. reed, seed** | |
| **5. bid, Sid** | |
| **TOTAL** *(5 possible)* | |

**Blending**

| Item | Answer | Score (0,1) |
|---|---|---|
| 1. /hot/ /dog/ | hotdog | |
| 2. /barn/ /yard/ | barnyard | |
| 3. /sleep/ /walk/ | sleepwalk | |
| 4. /trav/ /el/ | travel | |
| 5. /mag/ /ic/ | magic | |
| | **TOTAL** *(5 possible)* | |

## Set 10 — Required

| Listening Comprehension | Score (0,1) |
|---|---|
| **1. How do you think the bird got the ribbon?**<br>Answer: Amy lost it/dropped it and the bird found it. | |
| **2. Why does Amy's mom take her to Sam's shop?**<br>Answer: To get a haircut and a new ribbon. | |
| **3. What does the word *curious* mean in the sentence, "Amy continued to walk home, but was *curious* about the pink ribbon in the nest." *curious***<br>Answer: Wanting to know about something. | |
| **TOTAL** *(3 possible)* | |

## Set 10 — Optional

| Rhyming | Score (0,1) |
|---|---|
| 1. lot, pot | |
| 2. tool, fool | |
| 3. fun, sun | |
| 4. slow, throw | |
| 5. fit, kit | |
| **TOTAL** *(5 possible)* | |

**Blending**

| Item | Answer | Score (0,1) |
|---|---|---|
| 1. /bed/ /room/ | bedroom | |
| 2. /cook/ /book/ | cookbook | |
| 3. /de/ /fend/ | defend | |
| 4. /cra/ /ter/ | crater | |
| 5. /rob/ /in/ | robin | |
| | **TOTAL** *(5 possible)* | |


Paul H. Brookes Publishing Co., Inc. 1-800-638-3775 www.brookespublishing.com

## Set 12 — Required

| Listening Comprehension | Score (0,1) |
|---|---|
| **1. In the story, who is Ms. Montero?**<br>Answer: Michael's teacher. | |
| **2. Where would Michael meet his mom after school?**<br>Answer: By the big tree on the playground. | |
| **3. What does the word *strolled* mean in the sentence, "They *strolled* past the little store and the gas station." *strolled***<br>Answer: Walked. | |
| **TOTAL** *(3 possible)* | |

## Set 12 — Optional

**Blending**

| Item *Pronounce letter sounds* | Answer | Score (0,1) |
|---|---|---|
| 1. /su/ /per/ | super | |
| 2. /ta/ /ble/ | table | |
| 3. /s/ /ad/ | sad | |
| 4. /r/ /at/ | rat | |
| 5. /h/ /ot/ | hot | |
| | **TOTAL** *(5 possible)* | |

## Set 14 — Required

| Listening Comprehension | Score (0,1) |
|---|---|
| **1. What do you think might happen the next time the dogs' owner goes to work?**<br>Answer: Duke and Maddy will jump the fence again and look for the place called "work." | |
| **2. Why do Duke and Maddy think work is a wonderful place?**<br>Answer: They found food and they think "work" is a place with wonderful food. | |
| **3. What does the word *instantly* mean in the sentence, "They followed a man into the building and *instantly* smelled food." *instantly***<br>Answer: At once; to happen right away. | |
| **TOTAL** *(3 possible)* | |

## Set 14 — Optional

### Blending

| Item *Pronounce letter sounds* | Answer | Score (0,1) |
|---|---|---|
| 1. /c/ /an/ | can | |
| 2. /l/ /ip/ | lip | |
| 3. /r/ /un/ | run | |
| 4. /b/ /a/ /t/ | bat | |
| 5. /t/ /o/ /p/ | top | |
| | **TOTAL** *(5 possible)* | |

### Segmenting

| Item | Answer | Score (0,1) |
|---|---|---|
| 1. am | 2 | |
| 2. fed | 3 | |
| 3. no | 2 | |
| 4. is | 2 | |
| 5. gnat | 3 | |
| | **TOTAL** *(5 possible)* | |

## Set 16 — Required

| Listening Comprehension | Score (0,1) |
|---|---|
| **1. What happened when Ray drew a river with fish?**<br>Answer: They became real and were in his backyard. | |
| **2. Why wasn't the chalk like ordinary chalk?**<br>Answer: It makes things you draw come to life or become real. | |
| **3. What does *nonstop* mean in the sentence, "The week Ray got the chalk it rained *nonstop.*" *nonstop***<br>Answer: To continue without pauses or stops. | |
| **TOTAL** *(3 possible)* | |

## Set 16 — Optional

### Blending

| Item *Pronounce letter sounds* | Answer | Score (0,1) |
|---|---|---|
| 1. /bl/ /ast/ | blast | |
| 2. /t/ /ip/ | tip | |
| 3. /m/ /itt/ | mitt | |
| 4. /l/ /a/ /p/ | lap | |
| 5. /b/ /a/ /ck/ | back | |
| | **TOTAL** *(5 possible)* | |

### Segmenting

| Item | Answer | Score (0,1) |
|---|---|---|
| 1. it | 2 | |
| 2. dog | 3 | |
| 3. on | 2 | |
| 4. fan | 3 | |
| 5. kick | 3 | |
| | **TOTAL** *(5 possible)* | |

## Set 18 — Required

| Listening Comprehension | Score (0,1) |
|---|---|
| **1. What made Megan plump?**<br>Answer: The brew. | |
| **2. Why wasn't Megan like most pigs?**<br>Answer: She was born skinny and couldn't gain weight. | |
| **3. What does *plump* mean in the sentence, "Megan wasn't like the other pigs in her family that were *plump*." *plump***<br>Answer: Having a full or rounded shape. | |
| **TOTAL** *(3 possible)* | |

## Set 18 — Optional

### Blending

| Item *Pronounce letter sounds* | Answer | Score (0,1) |
|---|---|---|
| 1. /r/ /ot/ | rot | |
| 2. /m/ /an/ | man | |
| 3. /f/ /l/ /o/ /p/ | flop | |
| 4. /c/ /a/ /p/ | cap | |
| 5. /s/ /o/ /n/ /g/ | song | |
| | **TOTAL** *(5 possible)* | |

### Segmenting

| Item | Answer | Score (0,1) |
|---|---|---|
| 1. so | 2 | |
| 2. red | 3 | |
| 3. off | 2 | |
| 4. sip | 3 | |
| 5. ad | 2 | |
| | **TOTAL** *(5 possible)* | |

| Word Reading | Score (0,1) |
|---|---|
| 1. it | |
| 2. fat | |
| 3. mad | |
| 4. cat | |
| 5. in | |
| **TOTAL** *(5 possible)* | |


Paul H. Brookes Publishing Co., Inc. 1-800-638-3775 www.brookespublishing.com

## Set 20 — Required

| Listening Comprehension | Score (0,1) |
|---|---|
| **1. What do you use a sinker for?**<br>Answer: As a weight to help the fishing line sink. | |
| **2. What does the person telling the story want to happen next summer?**<br>Answer: To catch a fish. | |
| **3. What does *attract* mean in the sentence, "We put the bait on the hook to *attract* the fish that like to eat shrimp." *attract***<br>Answer: To cause to draw near; to appeal to. | |
| **TOTAL** *(3 possible)* | |

## Set 20 — Optional

**Blending**

| Item *Pronounce letter sounds* | Answer | Score (0,1) |
|---|---|---|
| 1. /n/ /ot/ | not | |
| 2. /s/ /it/ | sit | |
| 3. /p/ /et/ | pet | |
| 4. /f/ /a/ /n/ | fan | |
| 5. /y/ /e/ /t/ | yet | |
| | **TOTAL** *(5 possible)* | |

**Segmenting**

| Item | Answer | Score (0,1) |
|---|---|---|
| 1. barn | | |
| 2. dig | | |
| 3. core | | |
| 4. big | | |
| 5. pan | | |
| | **TOTAL** *(5 possible)* | |

| Word Reading | Score (0,1) |
|---|---|
| 1. not | |
| 2. mat | |
| 3. sad | |
| 4. at | |
| 5. mom | |
| **TOTAL** *(5 possible)* | |

## Set 22 — Required

| Listening Comprehension | Score (0,1) |
|---|---|
| **1. Why did Jan have to move?**<br>Answer: Her parents had jobs that made them move. | |
| **2. What do you think Jan will do during recess time at her new school?**<br>Answer: Tell stories. | |
| **3. What does the word *imagine* mean in the sentence, "The other boys and girls in her class would sit around in a circle and *imagine* all of the places in her stories."** ***imagine***<br>Answer: To think of something in your mind that you don't know about. | |
| **TOTAL** *(3 possible)* | |

## Set 22 — Optional

### Blending

| Item *Pronounce letter sounds* | Answer | Score (0,1) |
|---|---|---|
| 1. /l/ /ap/ | lap | |
| 2. /f/ /ad/ | fad | |
| 3. /c/ /u/ /p/ | cup | |
| 4. /s/ /a/ /p/ | sap | |
| 5. /t/ /a/ /g/ | tag | |
| | **TOTAL** *(5 possible)* | |

### Segmenting

| Item | Answer | Score (0,1) |
|---|---|---|
| 1. torn | | |
| 2. rack | | |
| 3. top | | |
| 4. sack | | |
| 5. let | | |
| | **TOTAL** *(5 possible)* | |

### Word Reading

| Word Reading | Score (0,1) |
|---|---|
| 1. cut | |
| 2. add | |
| 3. lot | |
| 4. rod | |
| 5. am | |
| **TOTAL** *(5 possible)* | |


Paul H. Brookes Publishing Co., Inc. 1-800-638-3775 www.brookespublishing.com

## Set 24 — Required

| Listening Comprehension | Score (0,1) |
|---|---|
| 1. **Why doesn't the person telling the story want his/her dad to find out you can't catch rainbows?** Answer: He/She likes spending time with his/her dad and getting strawberry ice cream. | |
| 2. **What does the person telling the story and his/her cousins look for in the stars?** Answer: Pictures. | |
| 3. **What does the word *compare* mean in the sentence, "I really can't *compare* the two places because they are different worlds." *compare*** Answer: To describe the similarities and/or differences. | |
| **TOTAL** *(3 possible)* | |

## Set 24 — Optional

### Blending

| Item *Pronounce letter sounds* | Answer | Score (0,1) |
|---|---|---|
| 1. /b/ /a/ /n/ /k/ | bank | |
| 2. /l/ /e/ /t/ | let | |
| 3. /s/ /i/ /d/ | sid | |
| 4. /m/ /e/ /t/ | met | |
| 5. /p/ /a/ /n/ | pan | |
| | **TOTAL** *(5 possible)* | |

### Segmenting

| Item | Answer | Score (0,1) |
|---|---|---|
| 1. pat | | |
| 2. log | | |
| 3. wet | | |
| 4. mat | | |
| 5. fog | | |
| | **TOTAL** *(5 possible)* | |

### Word Reading

| Word Reading | Score (0,1) |
|---|---|
| 1. fit | |
| 2. hen | |
| 3. on | |
| 4. go | |
| 5. sit | |
| **TOTAL** *(5 possible)* | |